RUSSIA

A PORTRAIT

RUSSIA
A PORTRAIT

LEV POLIAKOV

Introduction by
JOSEPH BRODSKY

FARRAR STRAUS GIROUX • NEW YORK

Library of Congress Cataloging-in-Publication Data
Poliakov, Lev.
Russia : a portrait / Lev Poliakov ; introduction by Joseph
Brodsky.
p.   cm.
I. Soviet Union—Description and travel—1970– —Views.
I. Title.   DK18.5.P65   1991   947.085—dc20   91-15578   CIP

IN PRAISE OF GRAY

Countries used to change slowly. More slowly, at any rate, than people. Nowadays, however, a photograph taken twenty years ago often reveals a landscape that does not exist, features that have been altered.

This rule has fewer and fewer exceptions; even Russia doesn't qualify for one. In fact, Russia, with her quest for industrial, political, and every other kind of modernity, is very much a case in point. Replacing a horse-drawn wagon with a lorry ages a vista, not to mention a street, irreparably and at once. Then it is down to those lorries' succeeding models, to the evolution of silhouettes from the rectangular to the bulbous to the sleek. With every new make, a landscape gets less recognizable. In fact, new makes a country's facial marks, something by which one can make it out in the picture, tell its age. And often it's a country's very poverty that renders it, if not necessarily young, then at least aging well; and you linger before a photograph unable to determine whether it is Turkey or Venezuela. In a poor country which cannot afford new technology, old lorries die hard.

Everything leaves traces hardening into creases. The sound of rock-and-roll over a transistor radio, the white trail of something supersonic across the fathomless view above, a pair of sneakers wading in the spring mud of a country lane tell you that the country you once knew is gone. Had our photographer trained his lens on Russia today, a minimum of one-third of his frames' contents would be different. You don't need to be a Heraclitus to be unable to step in the same river twice, even if that river is just the Neva. A mirror alone will suffice; and it would be a surprise to find a river still there.

Two-thirds would remain intact. What you are looking at in this album is just that: the two-thirds that only a quarter century ago were the whole story. What's more, this was the place's whole story for most of this century, and then some before. The visual idiom of any country is determined by its soil and the tint of people's dwellings. For that reason, the photograph's black-and-white is highly congenial to Russia, since the realm is predominantly threadbare gray. A painter doing his landscape here in vivid colors would be obliging his métier rather than reality—unless, of course, he resolves to challenge it. A camera in these parts is a greater realist, so much so the wonder is that it wasn't invented locally. By the same token, it is the greater metaphysician.

For gray is the color of time; and time's wardrobe here knows very few changes. Water is gray; so, for months on end, is the northern sky. Gray are men's and women's jackets, overcoats, cloth caps, boots and trousers, wooden huts, the sheen of skin, pavements, tires, fences, roads in spring as well as in autumn, milk canisters, locomotives, cisterns, rails, nails, forks, knives and scissors, loaves of bread, cement, stucco, boiled meat, potatoes, shopping bags, earth, dust, tree trunks; often the very eyes. It is largely a monochrome country where everything merges quite unwittingly and the mind gets easily drowned in a common denominator whose nature is as elemental as it is political. The official red takes care of the whole spectrum, and the eye here is equally stunned by the predictability of the future of a peasant as a prisoner. And then it rains.

For a camera's lens, this place is a real safari. A great mistake for a photographer is to bring his color film here. The net result will be like Turner'd talkies or like a bald man's hairpiece: garish and forced. The virtue of the collection at hand is that it is pre-Kodak as

6

much as it is post-Kodak, for the country is old, vast, and obstinate enough to succumb to the flattery of chemicals. On the other hand, of course, its author had no choice. A quarter of a century ago this photographer himself was part of the landscape he was depicting, and the material he had at his disposal was manufactured by this country's equally gray extension: Agfa, in the DDR.

The outcome is not so much historical as it is existential. One turns these pages with an uneasy, almost embarrassing sensation—akin to that with which one might read the letters of the dead. Or else this album recalls those poorly framed, fading, housefly-peppered collages of kinfolk one sees in the villages or in the factory workers' city flats, with all those frozen moms and dads, the bulging eyes of the brother in the army or navy uniform in which he no doubt died, babies, weddings, classmates, mementos of visiting the capital. Two-thirds of those depicted are either buried or changed utterly; but here it is, the past.

A picture aids memory. By the type of bicycle, car fender, policeman's uniform, or women's shoes a Russian perusing this album will immediately recognize the late sixties, the beginning of the seventies. An American, on the other hand, will identify all this as the attire of the Depression. Both will be right, because the texture of the Russian seventies and the American thirties is quite identical, in the countryside especially. Should somebody have told that to the photographer and his subjects, they would have felt flattered. As for Americans, there are fewer and fewer who remember the Depression with any clarity. This album—not to mention whole regions of Russia even today—may come in handy to the students of both the period and the general fabric of life.

Apart from feeling flattered, had one been conscious of the aforementioned similarity at the time, one would have taken more pictures. Yet the reason one didn't was that a depressed state in the economy and in the human psyche was and in many ways still is and promises to remain the standard Russian condition. If this album nevertheless conveys some *joie de vivre*, it is because the chronically ill value small pleasures. Hence the intensity of sentiment in catching a silvery fish from the gray river, in winning at hopscotch, in making an overcrowded bus, or in watching it burn. The Russians are very observant people, very attentive to detail. At any given moment, they feel themselves individually and as a nation to be at the hub of the universe and take everything within their sight and earshot highly personally. Wrapped or, better yet, swaddled in themselves like their children in winter clothes, sharing the existential uniformity of a centralized state, they are ideal subjects for a photographer if only because each one—whether he likes it or not—is very typical, by social definition.

That's what makes this collection of pictures so poignant. In a decade or so, they won't apply—or will apply less. The wardrobe will expand, colors will become more prominent. The dark-gray cotton jacket, the military tunic, tarpaulin boots, white kerchief, cloth caps will be replaced with polyester, plastic, and rubber of the shades and patterns only these materials are able to conjure; buttons will yield to zippers. The hills of the Central European Elevation, of course, will roll gently eastward and darken in the evening as before, but the eyes of their dwellers will be changing color according, not to the sunset, but to the TV set's.

Only the snow will keep doing its job, as if hired by the champions of black-and-white photography. But everyone will be sufficiently deceived by glossy Polaroids about the nature of time and their own essence. We've seen this happen in the West; why should the East be exempt from the common delusion? Color breeds expectation and evidently can be manufactured without nature's agency. Why should the East enjoy the privilege of dodging the ultimate disappointment—let's say, at the sight of ashes? The knowledge of gray should be left to Zen masters, of black and white to the printed word.

In that respect, the album at hand is indeed a book. Of short stories? Simply a handful of letters? In any case, a book that time is about to close. It would do so even had the stories been much longer, had this book been a novel. For, as it is, we read this book in its future: we look at these faces, façades, fates, faiths, and fashions from their future. So it is just as well that these stories are short, that these letters are few: the sense of their loss won't be so great. And our photographer may even pride himself on easing time's conscience—provided, of course, it's got one. We may never know what happened to these characters. As one of them, I am pretty sure we won't: once black and white, always black and white.

Joseph Brodsky
April 1990

RUSSIA

A PORTRAIT

1. Leningrad, 1967

2. Ryazan region, 1965

3. Tikhvin region, 1964

4.   Pskov, 1965

5. Tikhvin region, 1962

6. Peter the Great, Leningrad, 1965

7.   "Nymph and Minotaur," Jackobson Ballet, Leningrad, 1972

8.   Krasnovodsk, 1966

9. Tikhvin, 1964

10.   Shishkebab stand, Krasnovodsk, 1966

11. Pskov, 1965

12.   Karelia, 1963

13.   Pechora Monastery, Pskov, 1965

14.   Siberia, 1969

15. Leningrad, 1967

16.   Poet Joseph Brodsky, Leningrad, 1965

17.   Leningrad, 1970

18.   Ryazan region, 1970

19. Victory Day, May 9, Leningrad, 1969

20. Tikhvin, 1963

21.   Leningrad, 1965

22.   Leningrad, 1969

23. Leningrad, 1967

24. Moldavia, 1967

25. Astrakhan, 1966

26. Leningrad, 1965

27.   Artist Natan Altman, Leningrad, 1965

28.   Leningrad, 1970

29.   Actress Marlene Dietrich, Leningrad, 1964

30.   Peasant market, Leningrad, 1964

31.   Carpathy, West Ukraine, 1968

32.   Issyk-Kul Lake, 1966

33.   Slantsy, 1969

34.　Tbilisi, 1964

35.   Ukraine, 1965

36.   Leningrad, 1968

37.   N. Akimov's funeral, Leningrad, September 1968

38.   Leningrad, 1967

39.   Bus stop, 1965

40. Black River, Karelia, 1965

41. Leningrad, 1970

42.   KGB prison, Leningrad, 1968

43.   Yuri Kartashov, Leningrad, 1969

44. Leningrad, 1962

45.   Poti, 1965

46.   Sokolniky Park, Moscow, 1965

47.   May Day parade, Leningrad, 1965

49.   Moscow, 1966

50.   Leningrad, 1969

51. Leningrad, 1967

52. Ryazan region, 1965

53.   Leningrad, 1971

54. Leningrad region, 1967

55. Pskov, 1965

56.   Peasant market, Leningrad, 1964

57.   Ryazan region, 1965

58. Guryev, 1966

59.   Peasant market, Moscow, 1970

60. Tikhvin region, 1964

61.   Lithuania, 1971

62.   Tikhvin region, 1962

63.   Fontanka River, Leningrad, 1970

64.   Poet Anna Akhmatova, Komarovo, 1964

65.   Kolomenskoye, Moscow, 1966

66. Black River, Karelia, 1965

67. Writer S. Volf, Leningrad, 1964

68.   Ryazan region, 1965

69. Moldavia, 1967

70. Antonina Kozlova, Leningrad, 1964

71. Leningrad, 1968

72. Astrakhan, 1966